Dave Phillips
GRAPHIC AND OP-ART MAZES

Dover Publications, Inc., New York

FOREWORD AND INSTRUCTIONS

Over the past few years there has been growing interest in mazes. This "maze craze" started in Great Britain and has begun to kindle interest in the United States. Although the revival is just beginning, the maze itself is one of the oldest and most beautiful of puzzles. I am happy to add my contribution.

I regard the maze as more than a mind-teaser. It is also an art form both in construction and in appearance. I dislike dead ends in mazes, so I have avoided using them in this book. I prefer to have you lost, struggling, twisting, turning in the maze, only to find yourself back where you started.

All the mazes in this book have solutions. In the simplest, you are required to follow a path from the start through to a goal without crossing a black line. This type of maze is best followed using something that will not mark the pathways, such as the eraser end of a pencil. Other mazes require you to travel through three or more sections without retracing your path. You will have to use pencil for this type, to keep track of where you have been; but if you lay tracing paper over the maze and mark your path on that, you will be able to use the maze any number of times. Instructions for other, special types of mazes are given where necessary.

Published in Canada by General Publishing Company,
Ltd., 30 Lesmill Road, Don Mills, Toronto, Ontario
Published in the United Kingdom by Constable and
Company, Ltd.

Graphic and Op-Art Mazes is a new work, first published by
Dover Publications, Inc., in 1976.

International Standard Book Number: 0-486-23373-1
Library of Congress Catalog Card Number: 75-46144

Manufactured in the United States of America
Dover Publications, Inc.
180 Varick Street
New York, N. Y. 10014

Number 1
Start in the center and find your way to the exit.

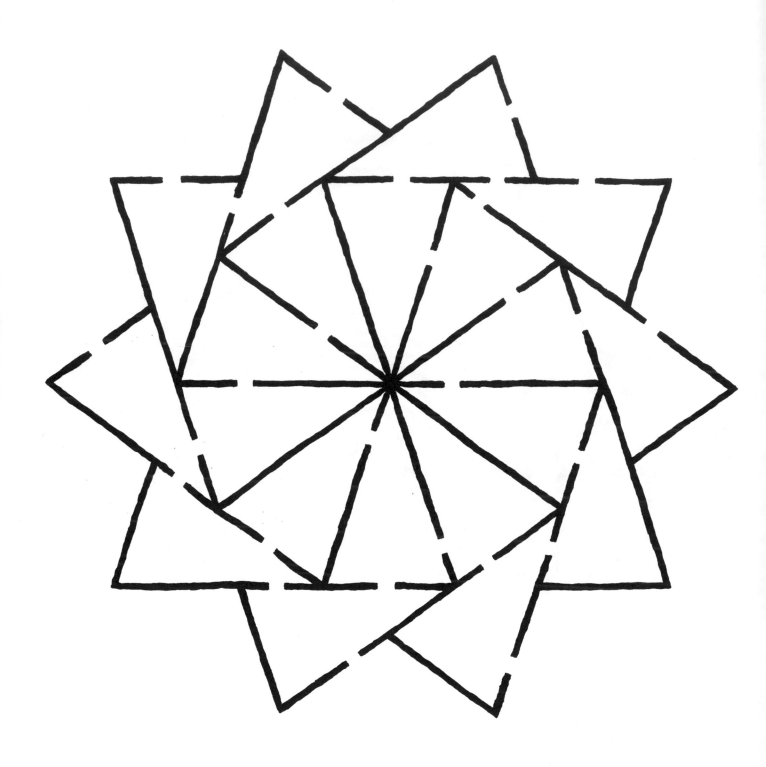

Number 2 (above)
There are twenty triangular compartments in this design. Start in any triangle you choose; finish in the same triangle, tracing a continuous path through each of the other triangles. You may enter a compartment only once and you may not cross or retrace your path.

Number 3 (opposite)
There are two white squares in this design, with four paths leading from each. Start in one square and travel to the other.

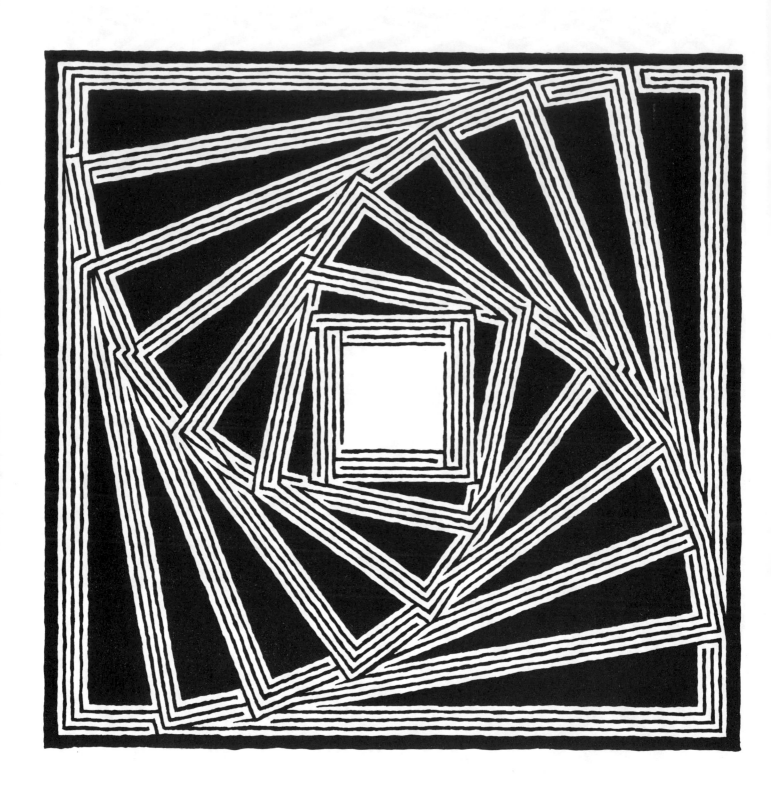

Number 4
Start in the center; find a way out.

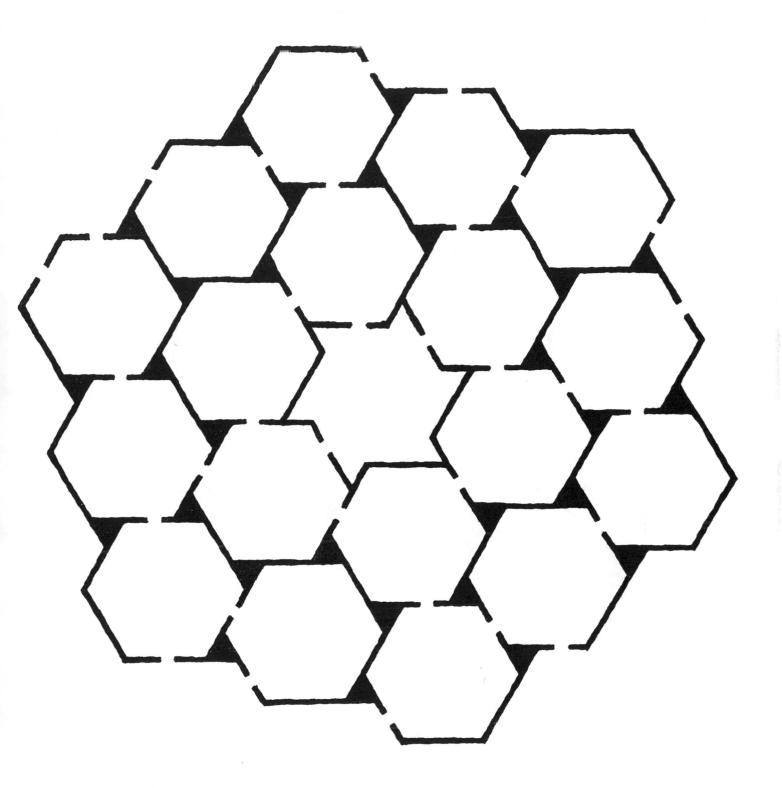

Number 5 (above)
Start in the center, travel through each hexagon only once and return to the center without crossing or retracing your path. You may not cross the center.

Number 6 (over)
This is a three-dimensional maze. The rotund gentleman wants to take his bath, but it is out of his reach. He must traverse a mountain of cubes before he can plunge in for, being a cumbersome fellow, he can only manage to step up or down one cube at a time. Help him find his way before the water gets cold.

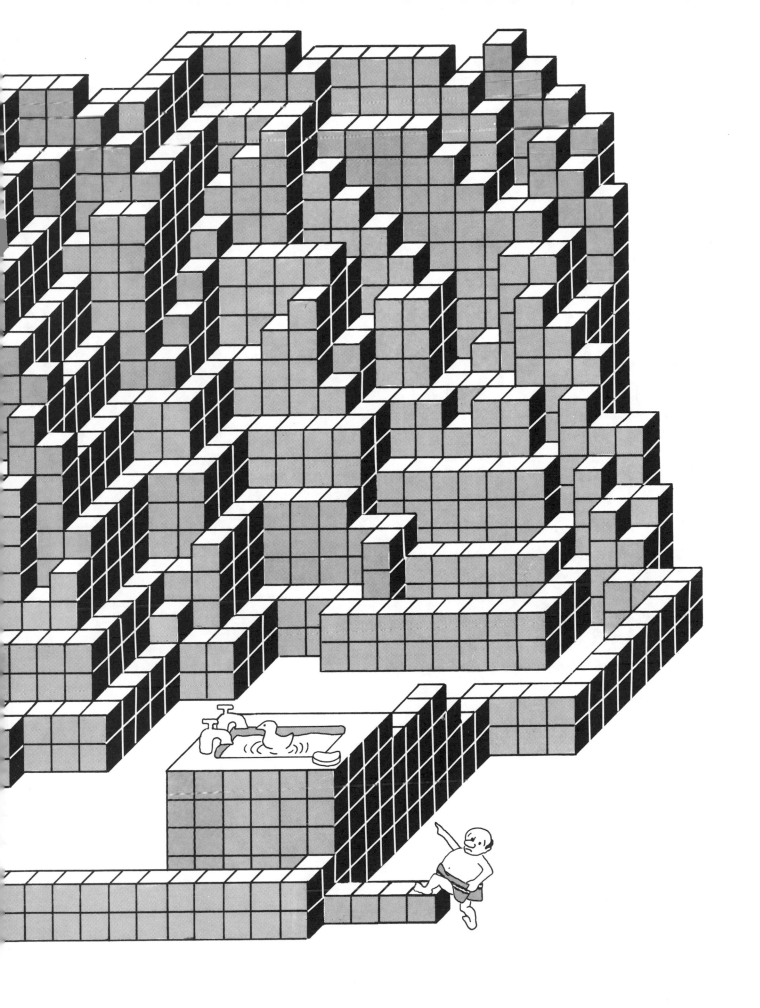

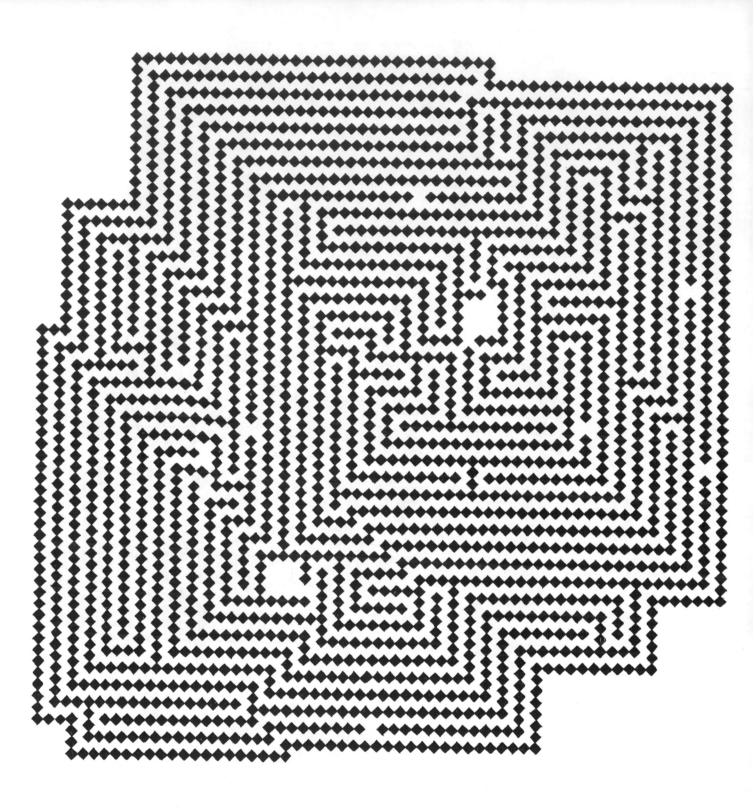

Number 7 (above)
Start in the top square; travel to the bottom square.

Number 8 (opposite)
Start in the center, taking either one of the two paths. Return on the other.

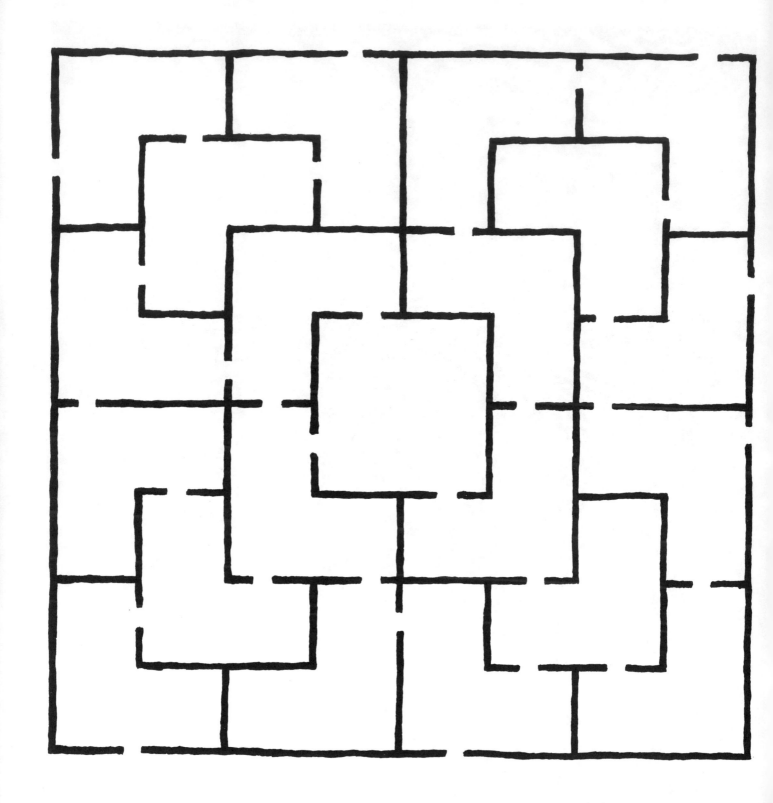

Number 9 (above)
Start in the center. Travel through each L-shaped compartment only once and return to the center. You may not cross the center during your journey.

Number 10 (opposite)
In these swirls there are two dead ends, one at the lower left, the other at the upper right. Start at one and travel to the other.

Number 11 (above)
Start in the center square. Visit the other four squares and return to the center without retracing or crossing your path.

Number 12 (opposite)
The enchanted vines. These plants share a common branch, so if you start at the trunk at the left and trace your way along the branches, with patience you will be able to finish at the trunk at the right.

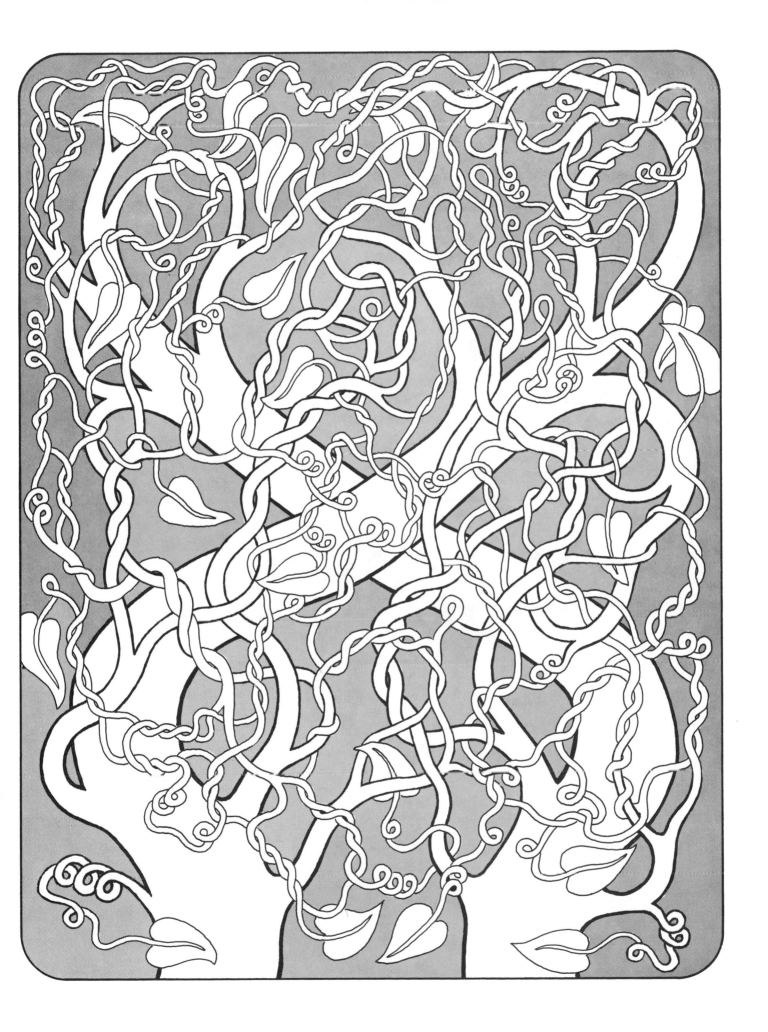

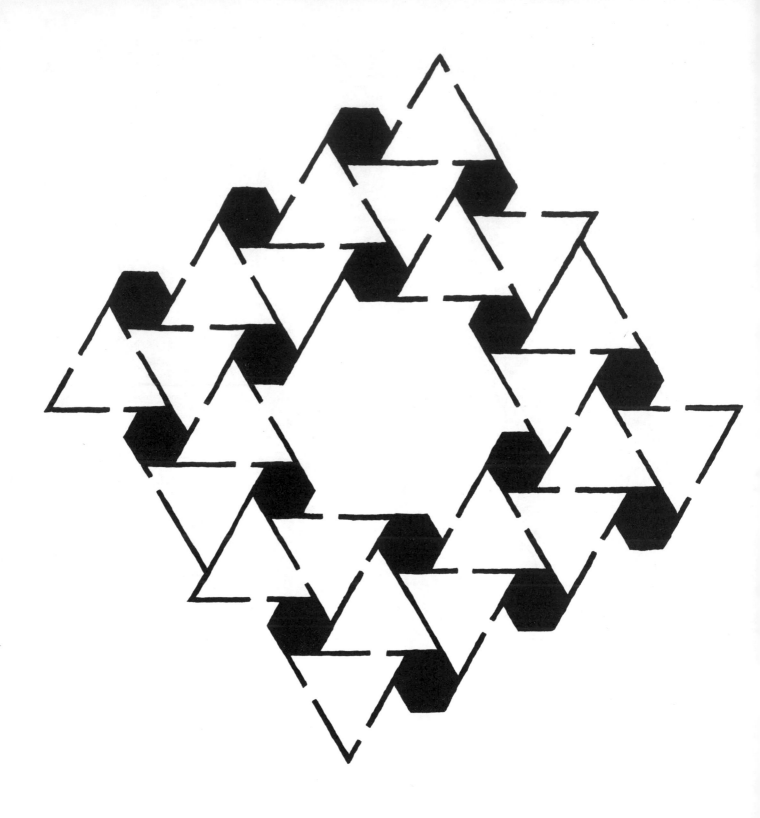

Number 13 (above)
Start in any triangle and finish in the same one without entering any of the other triangles or the center area twice or crossing your path.

Number 14 (opposite)
At first sight, all these colors may seem confusing. But if you can find the orange circle on the right and the purple circle on the left, you'll be all right. Travel the paths and watch them slowly change. Start is orange; finish is purple.

Number 15
Start in the yellow triangle; travel through the three orange triangles and return to the yellow triangle without crossing or retracing your path.

Number 16 (above)
Start is the green diamond; finish is the orange diamond.

Number 17 (over)
The Rainbow Maze. Start in the blue-green square on the left; finish in the yellow-orange square on the right.

Number 18 (above)
Start in the center; travel through each of the six other circles and return to the center without crossing or retracing your path. You will notice that the red and yellow paths blend into each other—this is all right. You may not, however, make an abrupt change across colors from red to yellow or vice versa.

Number 19 (opposite)
Starting from the center square, pass through each of the four outer squares and return to the center without retracing or crossing your path.

Number 20 (above)
Work from the purple center out.

Number 21 (opposite)
Find your way from the upper-left square to the lower-right square.

Number 22 (above)
Start at the center, pass through the three outer circles and return to center without crossing your path. This maze has many possible solutions; you need find only one.

Number 23 (opposite)
This is a three-dimensional maze. It is a structure of beams which, at first sight, may seem feasible to build. It isn't. Starting at the lower left, trace a path over the beams to the upper right. You may move on the top, bottom or side surfaces.

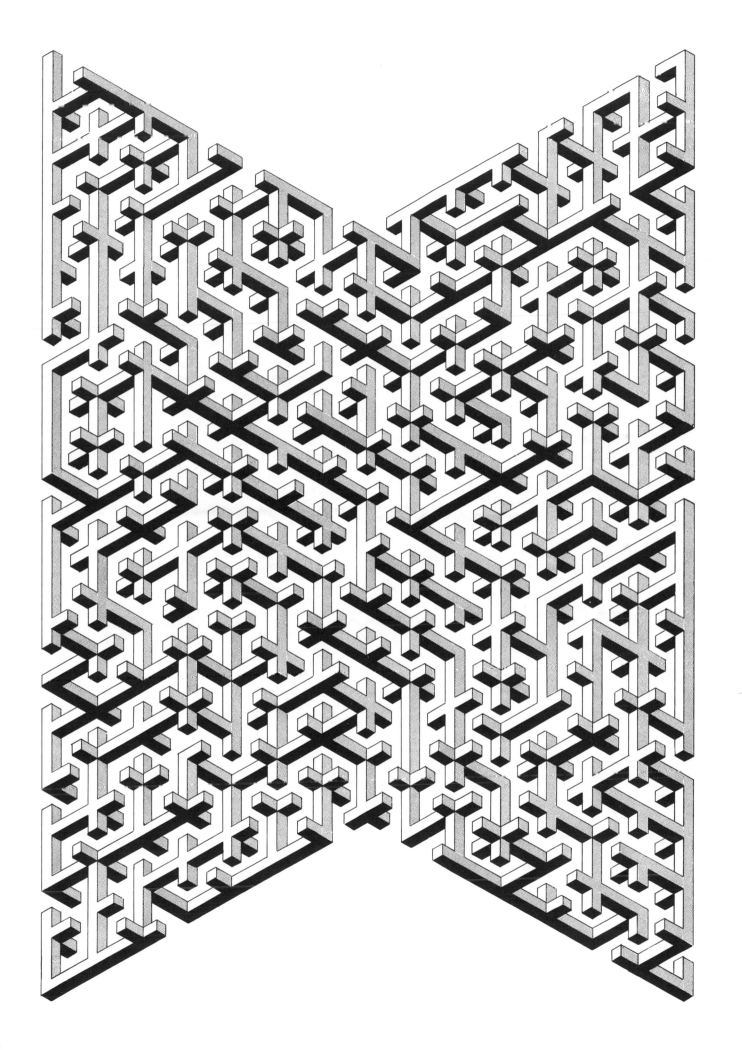

Number 24 (above)
The pentacle is devilish. Starting in the center circle, find your way to the five outer circles, then back to center, without crossing or retracing your path, or recrossing the center circle.

Number 25 (opposite)
This maze looks like the reflection in a pool into which someone has just tossed a pebble. Find your way from the bottom square to the top square.

Number 26
There are four squares in this design, one near each corner. Choose one of them to be both start and finish; travel through the others and return without crossing or retracing your path.

Number 27 (above)
Start in the center. Travel through each of the eight circles in any order and return to the center without crossing or retracing your path, or recrossing the center circle.

Number 28 (over)
Damsel in Distress. An evil wizard has abducted a fair princess and locked her up in a tower. Knowing that a handsome prince will try to save her, he has surrounded the tower with a labyrinth of stairs and hired an army of disagreeable cyclopes to guard it. "If the prince enters the labyrinth, he will surely perish," chortles the wizard. Fortunately, cyclopes are not known for their keen wit or quick reflexes. The prince may throttle a cyclops only from behind; to meet one face-to-face means certain death. If you step carefully, you will be able to reach the princess in her tower.

Number 29 (above)
Start in the center triangle, go through each of the circles and return to the center without crossing or retracing your path, or recrossing the center.

Number 30 (opposite)
Go from one square to the other. There are several ways of solving this maze.

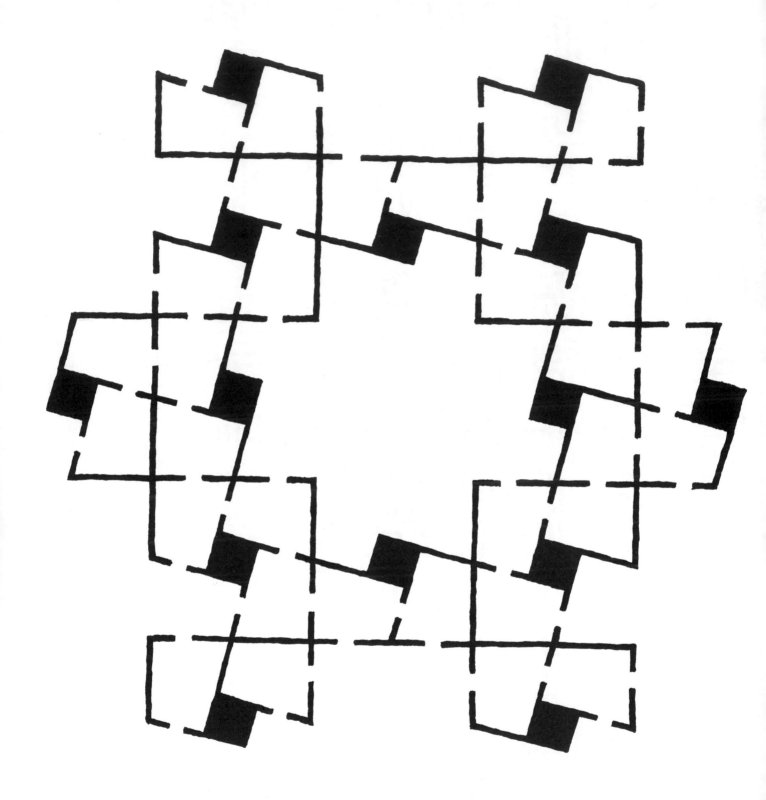

Number 31 (above)
Starting in the center, travel through each compartment only once and, without retracing or crossing your path or recrossing the center, return to center.

Number 32 (opposite)
Start in any circle, visit the other three and return to the first without using the same path twice.

Number 33 (above)
Start in the center, visit each circle and return to the center without retracing or crossing your path or recrossing center. There are a few solutions.

Number 34 (opposite)
Travel from the lower-left triangle to the upper-right triangle.

Number 35 (above)
Freeway One. The opening is both the maze's entrance and its exit. Follow traffic flow—you can't make U-turns or back up on entrance ramps. The lanes do not change under the overpasses.

Number 36 (opposite)
Freeway Two. This one is tougher. Use the same rules as in Freeway One, but enter at the top and exit at the bottom.

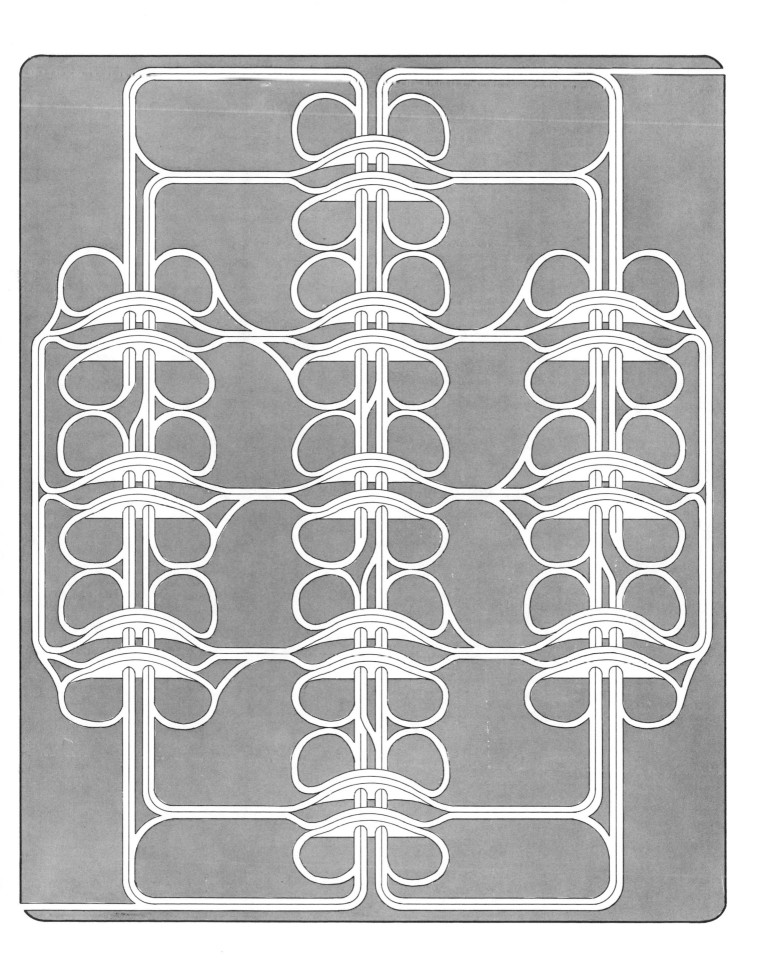

Number 37 (above)
All compassion fled from me when I designed this monster. The start and finish are in the center; you have twelve circles to visit without retracing or crossing your path. Nothing less than total commitment can solve it. You may not cross the center during your journey.

Number 38 (opposite)
Another horror! Starting at any one of the triangles, visit the other two and return to the first without crossing or retracing your path. The dead ends along the edges are only there for the sake of the design. If you wind up there, you have no one to blame but yourself.

Number 39
Start in one of the circles and visit the others without retracing or crossing your path. Finish in the circle from which you started.

Number 40
The last maze. Do you breathe a sigh of relief or of regret? Start at the center, visit each of the ten circles and return without crossing or retracing your path. You may not cross the center on your journey. I chose this as the last puzzle because it does not look too difficult. It may surprise you.

Solutions

The following pages show one (but not necessarily the only) solution for each maze. My sincerest congratulations to those few staunch souls who have, unaided, solved every maze in this book.

1

2

3

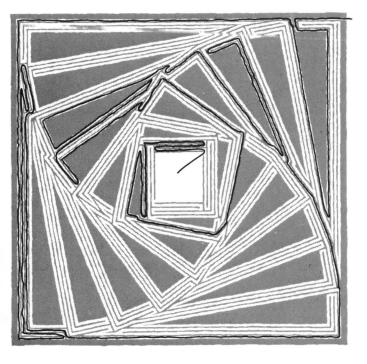

4

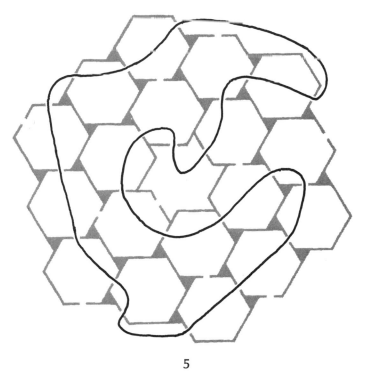

5

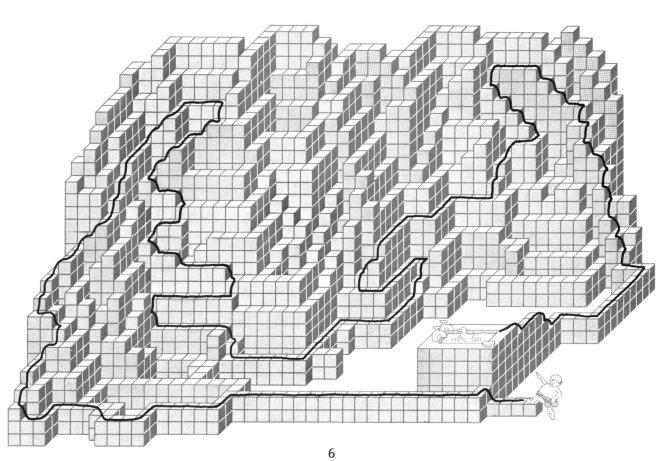

6

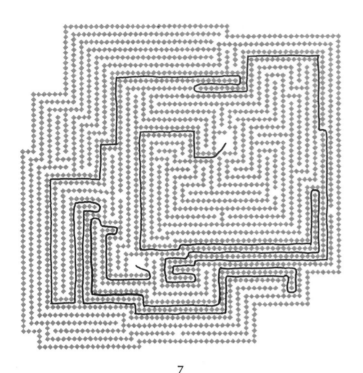

7

8

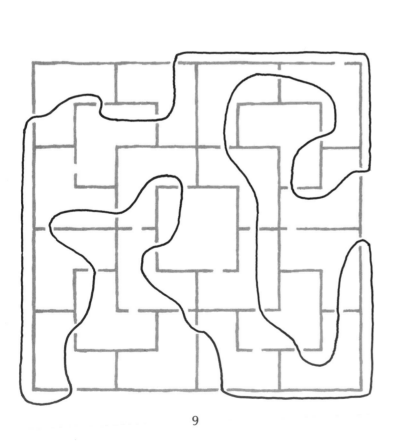

9

10

11

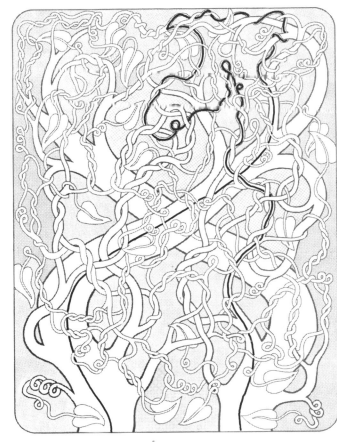

12

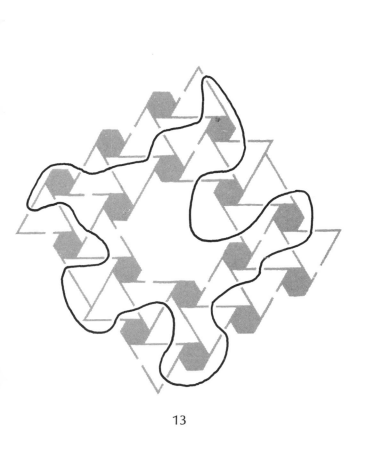

13

14

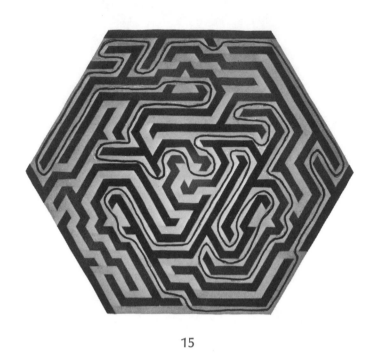

15

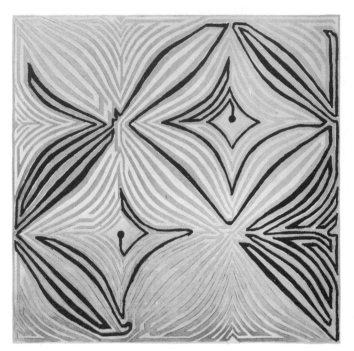

16

17

18

19

20

21

22

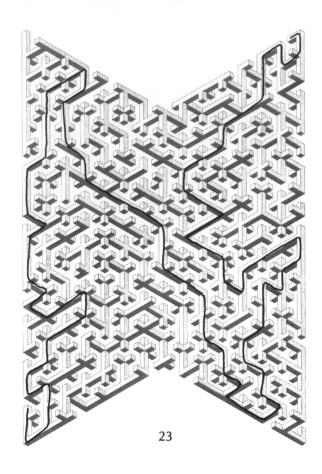

23

24

25

26

27

28

29

30

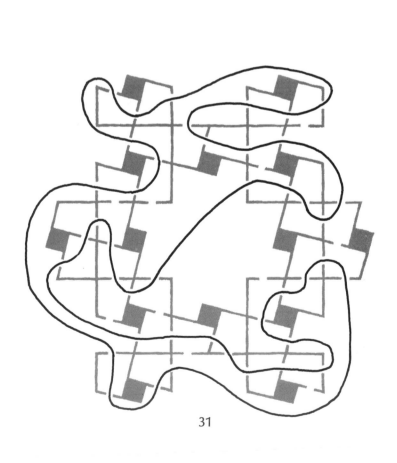

31

32

33

34

35

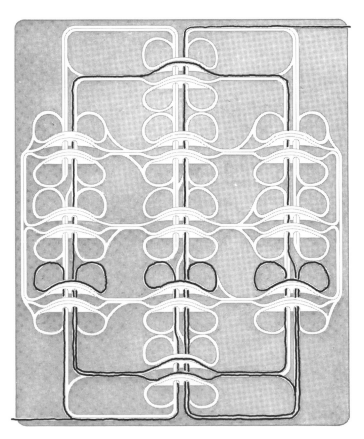

36

37

38

39

40